WATCH OUT!

WATCH OUT!

A Handbook for Safe Living

O.P. Mishra

NIYOGI BOOKS

Published by
NIYOGI BOOKS
Block D, Building No. 77,
Okhla Industrial Area, Phase-I,
New Delhi-110 020, INDIA
Tel: 91-11-26816301, 26818960
Email: niyogibooks@gmail.com
Website: www.niyogibooksindia.com

ISBN: 978-93-81523-75-9
Year of Publication: 2013
Revised Edition: 2019

Printed at: Niyogi Offset Pvt. Ltd., New Delhi, India

In the
loving memory
of my
parents

CONTENTS

V. P. Singh Badnore
Governor of Punjab
and
Administrator
Union Teritory, Chandigarh

सत्यमेव जयते

RAJ BHAVAN
Chandigarh

FOREWORD

I am pleased to learn that the second edition of the book ***Watch Out: A Handbook for Safe Living***, written by Dr O.P. Mishra, IPS, is going to be published. The English, Hindi, Konkani & Punjabi translations of this book have already been published. This in itself indicates the popularity and importance of the book for citizens in day-to-day life. We often fail to take some basic precautions in day-to-day life and become victims of crime. The author has very carefully selected every aspect of life that an ordinary citizen needs to go through as part of his daily routine. The safety tips mentioned in different chapters reflect the rich and varied experience of Dr Mishra. With development and technological advancement a normal citizen has become very vulnerable from personal security point of view. It is indeed pleasing to note that the author has included a chapter on cyber-related crimes and precautions to be taken by women & children in this regard. He has advised young children regarding dangerous online games like ***Blue Whale, Momo Challenge.*** The range of topics covered in the handbook is extremely comprehensive. Such a useful handbook can only be produced by an officer like Dr Mishra who carries with him an illustrious career of policing in different parts of the country.

In this age of increasing cyber crimes, it is incumbent on the government to devise ways and means for the protection of citizen's life and property. It is therefore, a responsibility of every citizen of India to contribute to Government of India's campaign of "Ek Bharat Shreshta Bharat" so that the people at large are aware of these issues related to security and safety in the national interest. This handbook is one step towards this direction.

This is a handbook which every family should read. The clarity of thoughts, simplicity of style and the manner in which this handbook has been organized, is indeed very impressive.

I wish Dr Mishra, all the very best in his future endeavours and look forward to more books being published by a versatile, service-oriented, thinking police officer like him.

[V.P. Singh Badnore]

THE CONTEXT

Policing is an institutional response to the various needs of citizens revolving around personal safety, security, law and order, prevention of criminal activities and maintenance of peace and tranquillity in society. In the more than three decades of my policing career in metropolitan areas, such as Delhi, Goa and Chandigarh, I have always tried to involve the community in day-to-day policing and have sought their trust and confidence. The basic objective was to keep the community informed of the latest crime trends and the precautions and measures to be adopted by them in day-to-day life to prevent crime. This was done through regular interactions with collective bodies. This handbook is an embodiment of those stray thoughts on the prevention of crime in certain critical areas of life in a more organised, structured and concrete form.

The English edition of this book came out in the year 2013. It was launched in Goa. It received very good response from people in general. The utility of the book for a common man was highlighted by media in their reviews. Keeping in view the broad contents of the book and its outreach to all sections of society, it was picked up by Department of Official language, Government of Goa for translation in the Konkani language. The Konkani translation was published in the year 2016. The books were distributed in all the schools in Goa. On my return to Delhi I translated the book in Hindi and the same was published by Niyogi Books in the year 2017. During my posting in Chandigarh, Sahitya Academy Chandigarh translated and published the book in Punjabi language in the year 2018. I would like to thank Directorate of Official Language, Government of Goa and Sahitya Academy Chandigarh for Konkani and Punjabi translations of the book, respectively.

The English edition of the book is out of print. The publisher wanted to include for any additions before publishing the second edition. The overall security scenario in general and dimensions of personal security has undergone changes since 2013. The vulnerability of citizens to cyber-related crime has increased manifold and poses major challenges before the law enforcing agencies across the globe. With more and more use of Internet for availing various services in day-to-day life, people are becoming victims of this anonymous crime. Our younger generation has exposed themselves to the evil design of cyber criminals on the net knowingly or unknowingly. The emergence of various social media platforms and chatting sites have made women, young girls and adolescents vulnerable to an unprecedented level of harassment online. Facebook has on record admitted few years back that it was the target of 600,000 cyber attacks every day. Children have committed suicide while playing online games like Momo and Blue whale. Women and children have become victims of child pornography, online fake marriages, cheating, fraud, impersonation, threat, blackmail, humiliation, social ostracism, etc. According to a recent UN Report: 'Combating Online Violence against Women and Girls: A Worldwide wakeup call', almost three-quarters of women online are exposed to some form of cyber violence worldwide and only 26% of law enforcement agencies in 86 countries surveyed are taking appropriate action. India is one country where reporting of cyber bullying is low. Only 35% women in India reported their victimization while a large majority 46.7% did not report.

While revising the first edition, I have included separate chapters covering different dimensions of cyber-related crime and precautions to be taken. There is a separate section on the recently launched Cyber Crime Online Reporting Portal started by Ministry of Home Affairs, Government of India.

While updating the handbook I went through the official websites of various national and international police organisations as well as reports and records. I would like to acknowledge all these organisations.

I would like to thank the Hon'ble Governor of Punjab and Administrator UT Chandigarh, Shri V.P. Singh Badnore for writing the Foreword of the second edition. I would like to especially acknowledge the contribution of my sons, Abhishek and Abhishank, for the correction of the initial drafts, meaningful inputs and critical comments, which helped in further enriching the handbook. Arti, my wife, was always there to encourage and support me in my academic endeavour.

Views expressed in the book are personal.

Dr O.P. Mishra, IPS

PROLOGUE

In the early phase of human civilisation, people used to move from one place to another in search of food and shelter. These groups carried stones and other handmade tools to protect their lives and belongings from unknown enemy groups. In the absence of codified laws, any deviance and criminality would be handled through collective decisions, conventions or social norms and mores. However, human beings could not afford to continue like this for a long time. As civilisation progressed, urbanisation and industrialisation changed societies. The overall development was visible through technological advancement. There were changes in governance and other socio-political and economic institutions.

Yet crime continued, though its methodology changed. It is against this backdrop that we should view the growth and evolution of socio, economic and political institutions.

Technological changes and economic advancement increased the level of happiness and prosperity in society. These changes had two far-reaching implications. At one level, it led to the emergence of a class of people that acquired maximum resources for its survival—the affluent. Simultaneously it produced another class of people who had minimal and inadequate access to economic resources for their survival. Unfortunately this gap widened beyond imagination across the globe over a period of time.

The overall dialectics of development also adversely affected the interpersonal relations of both these groups over a period of time. Latent hostility developed towards the affluent group by the underprivileged, which manifested itself in the form of crime. This problem became more acute in the middle- and low-income countries. The emergence of slums and unauthorised settlements and the culture of violence and crime need to be seen in this overall paradigm of development. However, this only explains a larger section of criminal activity. It does not cover those who have a tendency to commit crime owing to other genetic and non-economic factors.

Increasing crime in various forms has become a major challenge for law-enforcing agencies everywhere. In India especially, street crime in various forms has emerged as a daunting task. Preventing such crime, which creates panic in the minds of peace-loving citizens and providing material to electronic and print media for creating fear of crime, has become the yardstick to evaluate the overall performance of the police. Maintenance of law and order and prevention of crime will always remain the focus area and basic responsibility for policing throughout the world.

Policing requires the participation of other stakeholders in which the citizens play a crucial role. In a sense it becomes a participatory perspective in which the individual himself becomes a major player around whom everything revolves. It is a paradox that individuals in society have always looked at their own safety and security in a detached manner, assigning them a secondary role, despite the fact that the sufferer is the individual himself. Reasons for his own security and safety are assigned to the police who are always overburdened with other miscellaneous responsibilities. We must understand that a little bit of concern towards our own safety and security can save us from major tragedies in life. After all, ultimately we are the losers. A very famous author Robert Kiyosaki has rightly said the only person who is going to give you security and the life you want is you.

It has been rightly observed that crime is a threat to freedom and democracy. Reducing crime is imperative for stability, security and development. Crime cannot be totally eliminated, but a society with an effective system of governance can hope to reduce the incidence of crime to reasonable limits and to manage the detection and punishment of crime in an effective manner in order to maintain rule of law (Ministry of Home Affairs, July 2007, Report of the Committee on Draft National Policy on Criminal Justice).

The focus of this handbook is to highlight those critical areas related to safety and security of our property and lives where a proactive role played by the community and the individual can prevent crime in the long run. Basically the private security of an individual is affected at two levels: while he is inside the house and while he is on the move. He could be on his way to office, home, simply having a stroll, and so on. These are the times when he can be subjected to mugging, snatching, robbing or carjacking. Such incidents create panic and fear in the minds of ordinary citizens, especially women, children and senior citizens. They reflect signs of lawlessness and depict a very poor image of the local police. While individual security requires a more proactive role of the citizen, the police play a very important role in preventing street crimes.

Policing on the road is the core responsibility of the law-enforcing agency whereas policing inside the house must be done by citizens. In the long run, it is the perfect balance, cooperation, coordination and blending of private and public resources that prevent crime in a locality.

Watch Out! A ***Handbook for Safe Living*** identifies concrete forms of street crimes and crimes that happen inside houses and provides some basic tips to prevent these. It also covers target groups such as women and children, who are often victims of crime.

While talking about the safety tips discussed in Chapter 17, I would like to clarify in the beginning itself that various suggestions should be seen in the overall context of rapid urbanisation, greater social mobility of women in different walks of life and the social process which has increased the vulnerability of women to various forms of crime, particularly in metropolitan and big cities. These tips do not project any gender bias or reflect a typical mental construct which offends the sensibilities of women. I strongly believe that various forms of crime against women are essentially a reflection of a typical patriarchal mindset and attitude that denounce the basic tenets of gender equality and prescribe different parameters for living based exclusively on the basis of sex. Prevention of crime against women requires a radical ideological and attitudinal change in our perception towards women including officers and men in khaki who enforce various laws related to women.

Essentially, this book reflects my professional experience of more than 30 years in handling various criminal cases in a city such as New Delhi, Andaman & Nicobar Islands, Goa and Chandigarh. I hope it will help in preventing crime as well as increase the confidence levels of those who read it.

Dr O.P. Mishra, IPS

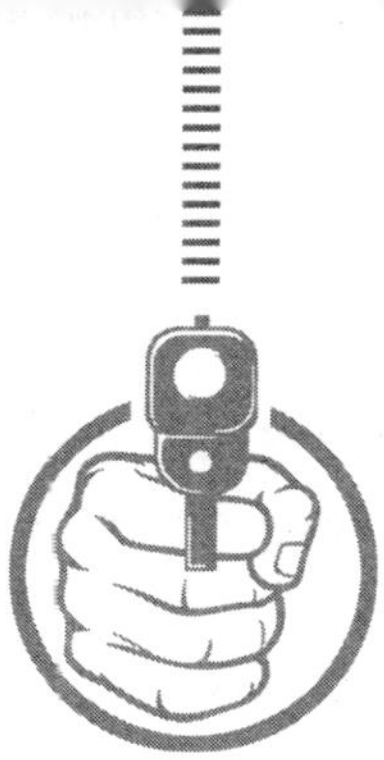

1

TIPS FOR PREVENTING TERRORIST ATTACKS

Terrorism is one of the major problems and challenges in the world today. Most of these incidents happen in crowded places in the cities. Yet, every terror incident can only take place through proper planning, cooperation, coordination and identification of targets. That normally does not happen in a day. It takes months to mobilise the resources, infrastructure and logistics. After all, a terrorist requires a place to stay and operate. While the prevention of terrorism requires a global strategy on different fronts, certain basic precautions by the key stakeholders (citizens, guest house staff, market associations and so on) who are also the likely targets could prevent such incidents.

General Citizens and Landlords

- Keep in mind that any suspicious person or activity could be a risk to you and others.
- Do not touch unclaimed objects.
- Immediately inform the local police or dial 100 if any suspicious object or unclaimed bag is located at a marketplace, in a bus, train or any other crowded place.
- Stay away from the suspicious object and keep others away as well till the arrival of the relevant agencies.
- Always establish the exact credentials of the tenant before renting out your premises.
- Insist on genuine documents related to identity.
- Inform the local police regarding the tenant.
- Any person offering exorbitant rent that is more than the market price should be viewed as suspicious.

Taxi/Auto Drivers

- Keep a watchful eye on your passengers and their luggage.
- Be suspicious if any car or two-wheeler is parked in your locality for days and the owner is not available. It could contain explosives with a timer device.
- Before buying a second-hand vehicle ensure that it is not stolen or wanted in any criminal case. Buy or sell cars, particularly second- and third-hand, after establishing the credentials of the buyer or seller.
- You can avail the toll-free services of your city police regarding information on stolen cars, including the national database of the National Crime Records Bureau (NCRB).

Guest Houses/Hotels Staff

- Keep a copy of the identity documents before checking in guests and install a CCTV camera for proper surveillance.
- Accurately fill up and submit all required forms to the concerned authorities.
- Do not allow the parking of vehicles beyond a particular period.
- Try to segregate the cars of clients and that of the hotel staff by designating a parking level for in-house transport.
- Use an effective access control system for all the gates of the premises.
- Install X-ray systems for the proper screening of baggage.
- Ensure the proper checking of vehicles entering the premises through inverted mirrors and undertake random checking of vehicles at the access points.
- Carry out anti-sabotage checks (such as cleaning of rooms) after a guest has checked out and before a new occupant enters.

Market Associations and Malls

- Proper parking systems should be organised for customers and shop owners.

- The cars of shopkeepers should be segregated from the customers by designating separate and exclusive parking labels covered under the authorised signatory.
- A CCTV system with recording facility for the surveillance of suspicious objects and persons is essential.
- Display the signage, 'You are under CCTV surveillance', outside the premises. It psychologically deters persons with ulterior motives.
- Associations should deploy chowkidars/guards outside their premises with designated beats for patrolling to keep an eye on suspicious objects/persons.
- Do not allow extension/unauthorised encroachment in any form outside a shop/establishment.
- Try to connect all shops with an alarm, which could be used by the neighbours for informing the police in case the premises are under any form of distress.

2

TOWARDS SAFE TRAIN TRAVEL

Crime in railways takes place both in running trains as well as while the train is stationary. As per *Crime in India* a total of 53 cases of Dacoity, 1,069 cases of Robbery and 33,682 cases of thefts were reported in trains. (National Crime Record Bureau 2016, p. 488).

- Always buy tickets from authorised agents and sources.
- Carry luggage chains and use them during the night.
- Do not allow any person without a ticket to travel in your compartment; inform the train ticket examiner (TTE) on duty. Insist (collectively) that the TTE/escort guard ensures that unauthorised persons move out of the reserved compartment.

- Accept eatables from authorised vendors only. Avoid anything offered by a stranger.
- Never expose your valuables or cash to fellow passengers. Don't open your bag that contains valuables such as cash and ornaments while travelling in public places.
- Never discuss the contents of your luggage with passengers.
- Do not reveal too many personal details to strangers.
- Do not entrust the custody of your luggage or valuables to any unknown person.
- Always identify unclaimed luggage or objects and immediately notify the police or a train attendant.
- Ensure that your luggage is latched and locked. Secure your luggage with a chain lock. Do not leave it unattended.
- Don't wear expensive ornaments while travelling alone.
- Use the 'train pulling chain' if required.

3

WHAT TOURISTS NEED TO WATCH OUT FOR

Tourists have to take special care as they are in a place where they are not aware of the people, customs, roads and so on. This is more so for foreigners...who are often, literally, taken for a ride! It is best to be alert at all times for statistics reveal that crime among tourists is rampant across the world.

- Always opt for a prepaid taxi or any other authorised mode of transport as soon as you arrive.
- Do not avail of transport, accommodation or any other form of hospitality from a stranger or a tout.
- Insist on the identity (address, telephone number) of persons who facilitate services for you.

- Do not ever buy tickets—train, air, sightseeing—from unauthorised persons.
- Be suspicious about persons who extend undue favours and courtesy even without your asking for it.
- Always use authorised transport services for sightseeing or for all-city tours.
- Do not sit behind the driver if travelling in a car, as it could be easy for the driver to lock the rear passenger door. Try to sit on the adjacent seat.
- Always book a taxi so that the identity of the driver can be established and traced.
- Disclose your itinerary for the day only to authorised persons on a need-to-know basis.
- Contact the local police on duty in the city for any help or information required.
- Advance planning on basics reduces your chances of becoming a victim of crime.
- Ask for details regarding directions, shopping or other things at the hotel/motel/guest house/place of stay. Looking lost makes you an easy target for criminals.
- Select only authorised guides at the monuments or other sightseeing places.
- Find out if there are any places in the city that need to be avoided. Always choose well-lit areas, particularly at night.
- Do not carry huge amounts of cash while on a sightseeing tour. Take only as much as you need.

4

WHEN DRAWING CASH FROM BANKS AND ATMs

Be careful while withdrawing cash from banks and ATMs. Criminals enter these premises as customers and choose easy targets after watching their activities in banks. While senior citizens and illiterate people have been cheated under the pretext of help by strangers, some have been robbed of cash outside their bank on the way to work or home.

- Preferably travel in a car/van with your security guard or an employee when carrying cash for the office.
- Keep information about cash, including transportation, date and time of movement, confidential. Share it only with concerned employees on a need-to-know basis.
- Keep an eye for any suspicious movement or strangers (on foot or a two-wheeler) in your vicinity.

- Do not follow the same route and timings when visiting banks and ATMs.
- Do not discuss cash or money transactions with strangers, or accept any offer of help from them.
- Do not get distracted by people who pretend that your money has fallen on the ground, inside or outside the bank.
- Do not authorise your minor children to withdraw large amounts of cash.
- When you type your PIN number at an ATM, make sure that you adequately obscure the keypad from being viewed by an onlooker. Be careful while withdrawing cash, particularly if someone is present in the premises.
- Ensure your privacy is not intruded upon while using the ATM. Make sure you log out in the right sequence. Do not forget to collect the card from the machine.
- Collect the cash and count it as unobtrusively as possible. Do not count cash while coming out from an ATM.
- Avoid using ATMs in lonely places, especially at night.
- Get your monthly pension or social security cheques sent directly to the bank for deposit. Try not to go to the bank at the same time each week.
- Put your wallet, money or credit cards in an inside pocket. Avoid carrying a lot of cash.
- Keep your cheque book and credit cards in different places. It makes it harder for a thief to forge your signature on cheques.
- When signing the bill counterfoil, after making a purchase with your credit card, make sure there are no duplicates or additional bills.

5

TECHNIQUES TO PREVENT IDENTITY THEFT

Safeguarding your identity is very important and today, with transactions taking place online and through credit cards, identity theft has become a major phenomenon. Globally, over 500,000 people are victims of this crime each year. The best protection always is prevention.

- Be careful of any document that has personal financial information and can give an identity thief a foothold into your life.
- Put all charge slip copies in a safe spot until your credit card bills arrive.
- After you have reconciled your bill, shred every statement, including credit card receipts, old bank statements, medical statements, everyday bills and pre-approved credit card offers.

- Write clearly on all credit applications. Consistently and completely fill in all credit and loan applications using your full name, first, middle and last. Every bill that comes to your house should be addressed in the same way.
- Monitor your credit accounts carefully, so you will know if a bill is missing or unauthorised purchases have been made.
- Close all unused credit cards. Cutting them up is not enough.
- Limit the number of credit cards you carry. The fewer cards you have, the easier it is to track them.
- If you are shifting residence, contact your creditors and update them with your new address immediately. You do not want credit information and new credit cards being delivered to the wrong address.
- If your credit card expires and you do not receive a new one, call the credit card company immediately.
- Do not provide your credit card number to anyone who contacts you on telephone.
- Make sure that online credit card charges are handled through a secure site or in an encrypted mode. You will know you are on a secure site if the web page on which you conduct your transaction begins with 'https' instead of the usual 'http'.
- Only shop on websites that offer a privacy policy. Know how your personal information will be handled. Print out privacy policies, warranties, price guarantees and other important information.
- Be watchful of shoulder-surfers. At ATMs and telephone booths, thieves will stand close enough to see numbers punched in by users.

6

HOW TO CHECK AUTOMOBILE THEFT

According to the National Crime Records Bureau approximately 27% of the total crime in Delhi itself is related to automobile thefts. Proper parking places can go a long way in preventing this.
During 2016, out of total theft (1, 94,558 cases), 74,293 cases (38.2%) were under auto theft cases of which Delhi (37,147 cases) has reported maximum auto theft cases followed by Bengaluru (5,843 cases) and Jaipur (5,271 cases).

- Install a GPS system, a gear lock, a steering wheel lock, a central locking system, ignition and fuel cut-offs.
- Install an alarm in the car and set it every time you exit the vehicle.

- Get the number plates of your vehicle etched on the windscreen and window panes.
- Always park your car in an authorised parking area.
- Never hand over the keys of your vehicle to the parking attendant. It could be used for making duplicate keys.
- Do a random check before parking your vehicle to ensure that no explosive is concealed in the parking area.
- When parking your vehicles in your house compound for the night, make sure they are locked.
- Do not park your vehicles outside your compound wall.
- If you notice an unattended and unknown vehicle parked in a certain place for a day or more, inform the local police, beat constable or the Control Room.
- Always hire a driver whose identity is established and keep a copy of his identity documents handy.
- In case your vehicle is stolen, inform the local police station as quickly as possible. Any delay will result in more crimes being committed and it will also increase the difficulty in tracing the vehicle.
- When buying a used vehicle, compare the registration, engine and chassis numbers with the RC Book (Certificate of Registration). Check the database of lost and found vehicles on the website.

7

SAFETY TIPS FOR THE ELDERLY

The number of older persons in India is expected to increase from 71 million in 2001 to 173 million by 2026.

According to *Crime in India* (NCRB) 2016: 21,410 cases were committed against senior citizens. Maximum senior citizens were victim of Cheating (1,941), followed by Murder (1,055) and Robbery (1024)–(p. XXI). The increasing norm of nuclear families, lack of proper social security measures, urban anonymity, alienation and egocentrism in the cities has led to senior citizens becoming vulnerable to crime not only in their homes but also on the streets. Lot of senior citizens are becoming victims of harassment, threat, intimidation, assault by their own children, primary and secondary relatives. They must know their rights as per the law.

- Connect your house to the neighbour's with an alarm bell.
- Keep important telephone numbers handy and save them in your mobile or some safe place in the house.

- Ensure police verification of your service providers. Take the services of only those recommended by the residents' welfare association.
- Keep in touch with the beat officer.
- Do not disclose your movements outside the house to everybody. It should be shared on a need-to-know basis.
- Secure your house with a magic eye and a door safety chain on the main door.
- Use strong iron grills for securing windows, doors, air-conditioners and coolers.
- Do not employ drivers and servants without verification.
- Always take someone reliable with you while drawing money from the bank.
- Never keep huge amounts of cash or valuables in the house.
- Establish the identity of the person before opening the door. Ensure that he/she answers your call.
- You can say no to any telephone sales pitch or just hang up on such calls. That is not being rude—that is taking care of yourself!
- Do not give your credit card or bank account numbers to people who call you, even if they say they are from the bank.
- If a stranger asks you to take money out of your bank account, don't do it. A thief can pretend to be a bank employee and ask you to withdraw money to 'test' a bank teller. Banks do not check their employees in this way.
- Deals that seem too good to be true are often rip-offs. Beware if you are asked to give someone a lot of money with the promise that you will get more money later. Check with your local 'Better Business Bureau' for more information about the record of any company before you do any business with them.
- Be on guard about hiring people who go from door-to-door looking for home repair work. They may not be trained to do so and may overcharge you. Try to get referrals for home repairs from friends and family. Always be very clear about the details of the work you want done. Never pay for the whole job in advance.

Safeguards for the Elderly Under the Law

Parents cannot be evicted from a house without the due process of the law.

Under Section 125 of the Code of Criminal Procedure (CrPC), a person who does not have sufficient means can claim maintenance from his/her children.

If children or relatives neglect or refuse to maintain a senior citizen who is unable to maintain himself/herself, they can be ordered to pay a monthly allowance to them under the Maintenance and Welfare of Parents and Senior Citizens Act, 2007.

The Hindu Adoptions and Maintenance Act stipulates that aged parents can demand maintenance from their children.

The Domestic Violence Act provides parents with the right to seek relief from any kind of abuse.

Based on the provisions of Article 41 of the Constitution of India and obligations under the various UN-backed international agreements, the National Policy on Older Persons (NPOP) was announced in January 1999. It identifies a number of areas of intervention–financial, healthcare, nutrition, shelter, education, welfare and protection of life and property–for the well-being of older persons. The National Council for Older Persons (NCOP) has been constituted to operationalise the NPOP.

Source: Rising Crime against Elderly Persons and Responsibility of Police in Metros: *Project report submitted to the Bureau of Police Research and Development, September 2009*

8

PREVENTION OF CRIMES RELATED TO SERVANTS

Domestic servants constitute an important service provider sector in our cities. However, over a period of time, many of them have been caught committing crimes at their owner's house, including robbery and murder. The investigation of servant-related cases reveals that they are often hired without any verification.

- Verify the credentials of your servant with the beat constable or police. A servant who is reluctant to get himself/herself verified may have malafide intentions.
- Obtain two references before employing a domestic help.
- Always hire a servant through a registered agency or someone known to you and check the details of the person who refers him/her.

- The permanent address can also be verified by sending a money order at your servant's home address.
- Ask for the name, address and telephone number of the domestic help's relatives and previous places of work.
- Keep a photograph and other details of your domestic help.
- Never expose valuables such as jewellery and cash in front of the servants or discuss their storage with them.
- Make surprise checks of their activities, particularly in the kitchen.
- Do not maltreat a servant.
- Think twice before re-employing a servant who was thrown out.

9

AVERTING BURGLARY AND HOUSE THEFT

While both these crimes can be prevented by adopting collective measures with the residents' welfare associations and the local police, certain steps taken by the residents themselves can go a long way in preventing such crimes.

1,11746 Burglaries and 4,94,404 theft cases were reported in 2016.

(Crime in India 2016, p. XXII)

- Do not keep cash and jewellery at home, especially if there is no one to guard it.
- Install electronic surveillance systems in your house with a recording facility.
- Alarms, CCTVs and door cameras act as invisible policemen.

- Secure your house with steel grills. Make sure that the window grills are not screwed into the frames, but embedded in the cement. Provide an additional grill where air-conditioners are fixed.
- Fix a metal grill or collapsible gate outside the main door. This will provide you visibility without exposing you to threats.
- Always keep your main door closed even during the day and secure it with a magic eye and a door safety chain.
- Ensure that the windows and doors are properly locked before you leave the house.
- Do not divulge your travel plans to strangers or leave a recorded message on your answering machine telling people that you are on holiday.
- Guards should be deployed in the area during the day and night through the residents' welfare association.
- Get to know your neighbours so that you can easily identify a stranger. Inform them if you plan to be away from home for a long or short period.
- Do not open the door blindly. Try to establish the identity of the person before letting him into your house. If at all you have to allow them inside when you are alone, call the watchman or a neighbour to stay around till the work is completed.
- Try to keep pet dogs, they serve well in guarding the house.
- Whenever you move into a new house, change the main door and back door locks.
- Ensure that your valuables, including mobile phones and wrist watches, are not visible from outside.
- Do not hide the keys of your cupboard where the valuables are kept in convenient places such as under the doormat or in a flower pot.
- Beware of persons coming to your house under the pretext of repairing, selling things or conducting meter readings.

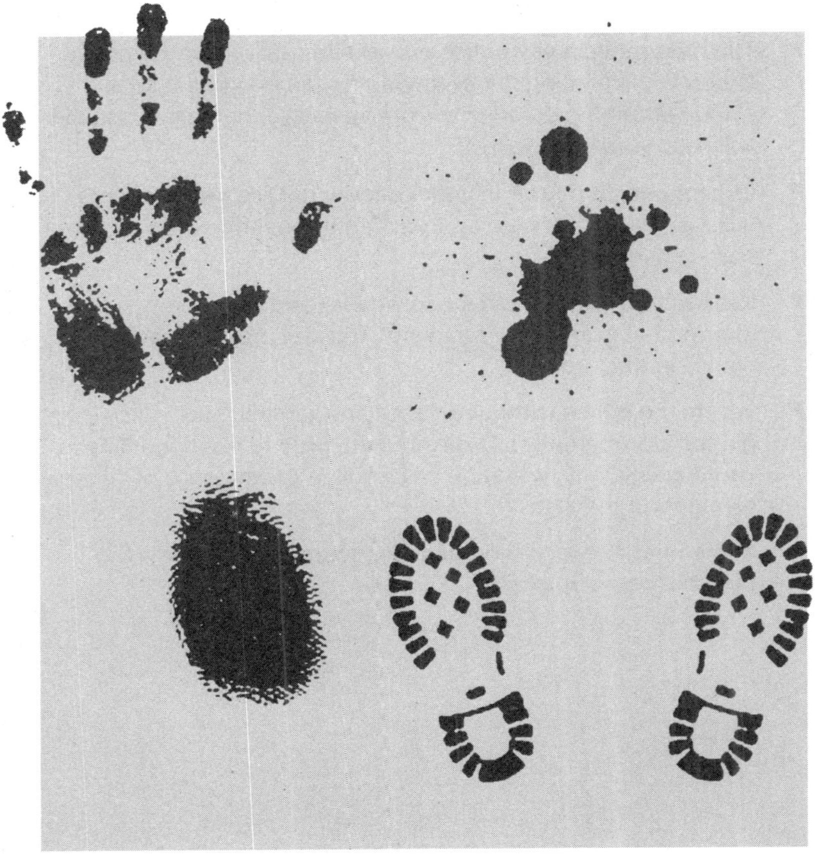

- If a theft has taken place in your house, wait for the arrival of the police and do not disturb the scene, otherwise it will lead to tampering of evidence such as fingerprints, footprints and so on.
- When you go out, switch on at least one inside light, to give the impression that the house is not empty and keep the outside lights on at night.
- There are timer mechanisms available in the market, which control lights. If you are planning to be away from home for some days, install one of these gadgets.

- The metropolitan city police provide free service to the public. When you are going out of town, you can inform the local station about the duration of your absence. The beat constables will keep watch regularly.
- Organise night patrols in your community. The local police will assist you if they are approached through the residents' welfare association.
- Keep in touch with the beat constables and keep them informed of even minor incidents. This will prevent major crimes in the future.
- Inform the police without delay of any gambling activities, pirated/pornography CD distribution, drug or illicit peddling in your locality. Any hesitation will result in the increase of criminal elements in the area.
- Remember, the more you deny the temptation, the less the threat of being burgled.

10

SAFE KEEPING OF VALUABLES

Your jewellery and important documents, especially those relating to your fixed deposits, property, inheritance and so on, are most valuable and it is imperative that you keep these safely. People who have been careless have often spent a lifetime recovering from huge losses!

- Keep jewels, important documents and other valuables in bank lockers. Bring them home only when absolutely necessary.
- Do not keep valuables or money in the side box of your parked two-wheeler.
- Women must conceal their neck jewels while travelling by public transport.

- If you are coming out of the bank after withdrawing cash or out of a jewellery shop after a purchase, be alert of somebody trying to divert your attention by pointing out to dirt or waste on your person, spitting betel nut on you or throwing some money on the street.
- Keep your valuables or money safely tucked away inaccessibly on your person while taking public transport.
- Do not respond to people offering to assist or those making sexual advances in public transport. These are some of the common diversionary tactics employed.
- The safest, inevitably, will be to avoid travelling in crowded public transport while carrying a lot of cash or valuables.

11

HOW TO CHECK CYBER CRIME

Cyber crimes take place because of extensive use of the internet and other IT-related services. Offences vary from tampering with documents and hacking into computers to fraud and breach of privacy. According to *Crime in India 2016*, a total of 12,317 cases of Cyber crimes were committed in the year 2016. Out of these 48.6% (5,987) cases were for illegal gain, 8.6% (1,056) cases were for revenge, while 5.6% (686) cases were related to insult to modesty of women (p. XXII).

- Avoid e-mails which claim: huge funds being deposited/ transferred into your account; a lottery won or a cash prize from a competition in which you never participated; a job abroad or a part-time job on a commission basis and a 'Will' made in your favour by a foreign-based, unidentified person.
- Do not send money or provide your user name/password to unknown persons.
- Cyber stalking results from people naively revealing too much information about themselves to identity thieves. Avoid divulging personal details.
- Watch out for anything that is weepy or intimidating. Document everything in order to help the police prosecute the stalker.
- If the stalker is known, send him/her a clear written warning to stop and never communicate again.
- Such communication should be saved in hard and soft copies.
- Collect all electronic and hard copy evidence of the stalker and document it.
- If the cyber stalking continues, complain to the Internet Service Provider (ISP).
- If someone uses your name, social security number or credit card without your permission it is a crime. This is known as an identity theft.
- The internet can give online hackers access to your computer, personal information and finances. You can reduce such crime by:
    - not responding to e-mails asking for personal information
    - being careful when buying things online (look for an address and telephone number and call the number to see if it works; only use websites of companies you trust)
    - using anti-virus and anti-spyware software and keeping your computer protection up-to-date
    - protecting your computer with a firewall. If you need help, ask someone who knows about computers to guide you
    - keeping your computer protected with a password

12

TIPS TO AVOID PHISHING

Phishing is an attempt to criminally and fraudulently acquire sensitive information, such as user names, passwords and credit card details, by posing as a trustworthy site in an electronic communication. Most online banks are common targets. Phishing is typically carried out by e-mail or instant messaging and often directs users to enter details at a website, although telephone contact has also been used at times.

- When you receive e-mails claiming to be sent by banking institutions asking you to enter your account details, do not do so! Your bank already has your details and clearly would not want them again.

- Do not respond to e-mails that seem like they have been sent from your bank. Some of the claims made in these e-mails may be as follows: you are to receive a refund; the bank is trying to protect you from a fraud or the bank needs some security and maintenance to update your account.
- If you receive such e-mails, always check with your bank directly or speak to the customer service representative.
- Never enter your credit card details and password in a website which you suspect is not genuine.
- It is a good practice to type in the URL of your bank yourself, or bookmark it if the URL is difficult to remember.
- Do not follow links to a banking website from another website or e-mail.
- Verify a website's URL before you provide your login details on any web page. Fraudsters create fake websites that have URLs closely resembling the original.
- Do not share your account details, password or credit card details with anyone whom you do not know or trust.
- Log in to your account regularly and look for transactions that you do not recognise.
- Do not send your account details and/or password over an e-mail to anyone, not even your family members.
- Check if the e-mail that you receive has your name correct. Do not open it if the spelling of your name is incorrect. Fraudsters try to guess your name by your e-mail address.

Take Care about Revealing Sensitive Information

Abhishek (victim) got an e-mail from a fake HDFC Bank that his account needed to be updated. When Abhishek clicked on the link provided in the e-mail (one must never do this!), it re-directed him to the fake HDFC Bank page. As the page was a lookalike of the HDFC Bank page, the victim entered his user name and password for his bank account along with all the details asked. Within a span of ten minutes, Rs 505,000 was withdrawn from his account by some unknown persons in six transactions. The amount was transferred to various accounts in HDFC branches across India.

Abhishek learnt the hard way that no genuine financial institution ever asks you to input any sensitive information.

13

WARNING SIGNS OF SPAM MAIL

Today a lot of people have access to internet and cyber cafes and are becoming victims of spam e-mails. The modus operandi for this is so convincing that anyone can fall into the trap.

- Beware of e-mails that promise to share or transfer millions of dollars to you. They will read something like this: 'Out of six billion people in the world you were singled out as this fortunate person, lucky you...!'
- The e-mail is usually marked 'urgent', 'top secret' or 'highly confidential' and demands that you act immediately. Time is commonly of the essence.

- The sender claims to be an exiled dignitary, cabinet member, CEO, CFO, lawyer, doctor or the heir of an important person to gain your confidence. These messages are usually sent through a free e-mail service.
- The sender claims to have got your e-mail address during a personal research on the internet or from an unidentified friend who was once on a diplomatic mission or from any other source.
- The proposal contains a seemingly unlikely situation, that is, overpaid millions on a contract, royal money or assets frozen by a foreign government, an inheritance or money, gold or diamonds that need to immediately transferred or they will be lost forever.
- The sender seeks an 'honest foreign partner' to help with the crisis, as if none exists or can be found in his own country.
- The message states that they are working with an unidentified security company or with the Central Bank of any other foreign country.
- A request is usually made for personal information from you, that is, your full name, bank account information and routing numbers, home or business telephone and facsimile numbers or a copy of your letterhead.
- The best tip is to delete any mail from a stranger which resembles the mails described above.
- The mail may be forwarded to the service provider's mail ID such as abuse@yahoo.com, abuse@hotmail.com.
- Similarly, you can forward the mail before you junk it to the local police e-mail ID.

14

HOW TO KEEP PASSWORDS SAFE

In the cyber world your password is the key to everything. It is best to keep it simple so that you can make a mental note of it and do not need to write it down anywhere. By simply memorising it, you also ensure that no one else knows your password.

- Keep in mind that your password is the secret that helps you to protect the valuable personal information that is stored in your computer and in your online accounts.
- Never share your password with anyone.
- Do not write your password on a piece of paper, send it via e-mail or share it with anyone over the telephone.

- Change your password regularly.
- Do not opt for the 'Remember Password' feature of applications for Outlook, Browser, Messenger and so on.
- Avoid typing the password in front of others.
- Always use different passwords for different logins.
- Use a password with mixed-case letters (for instance, AaBb) and use upper-case letters in the middle and/or end, not just at the beginning.
- Make sure that you use a password that is easy to remember, so you do not have to write it down.
- Use a password that you can type quickly, without having to look at the keyboard. This makes it harder for someone to steal your password by watching over your shoulder.
- Do not reveal a password in an e-mail message or over the telephone to anyone, not even family members.
- Do not talk about your password in front of others.

15

CYBER SAFETY FOR CHILDREN

Educating your children about the internet is the most effective way of protecting them against the dangers that lurk online. The naïve and trusting nature of children can make them an easy target for a variety of dangers on the internet such as bullying and harassment, pornography, information theft and financial fraud.

- Set the rules for internet use. Limit the number of hours and times at which they can be online.
- Install both commercial and free software that creates a safety system for your computer.
- Place the computer in a neutral space in the house such as the living room.

- Encourage your children to inform you immediately if they are threatened, scared or made uncomfortable by someone or something online.
- Guide them to be cautious about believing what they read on the internet because it is not always true or reliable.
- Tell them to be careful when they visit chat rooms and to keep out of chat rooms for adults under all circumstances.
- Instruct them to make sure that the firewall software is always running when they use the internet connection. Under no circumstance must this be switched off.
- Instruct your children not to give their own or their friends' names, addresses, telephone numbers, school names or other personal information to anyone online.
- Warn them that they must not send pictures of themselves, their parents or their friends to anyone without your permission.
- Do not allow them to fill forms or questionnaires online without your permission.
- Tell them not to visit websites that charge for services without your permission.

How to avoid your child becoming a victim of e-mail offences

- Take the child into confidence and get the information of the e-mail ID from where offensive e-mails are received.
- Save the e-mails, do not delete them from the inbox—there is a tendency to delete immediately when such e-mails are received.
- The ISPs normally preserve log details for a very short duration, which may vary from fifteen days to two months. Therefore, do not delay in approaching the police. It may result in evidence getting lost.
- Submit e-mail printouts with the full header along with the complaint to the police. Do not reply to unknown e-mail IDs.

How to avoid vulgar e-mails

- Various service providers allow the creation of personal profiles, but unscrupulous elements can misuse this, especially if a girl has a difference of opinion or a misunderstanding with a male friend. The male friend or his friends create vulgar/obscene profiles of the girl and post it on such websites along with the telephone number. The girl may then receive obscene and harassing telephone calls from all over the world. In such a case, enquire with the people who are calling to identify the ID of the profile so that it can be removed by requesting the website administrator.
- Take a printout of such a profile and submit it to the police.
- Service providers do keep records for the mandatory period. If objectionable MMS clippings are received, contact the police/ cyber crime investigation cell immediately.
- Whoever transmits obscene or vulgar messages commits an offence. For instance, if 'A' transmits to 'B' and 'B' to 'C' then 'A' and 'B' have both committed an offence. So do not transmit any message that is vulgar.

Parents must watch out for

- The amount of time your child spends on the internet, especially if this is late at night.
- Your child becoming secretive or defensive about his online activity and quickly changing the screen when you enter the room.
- Unusual charges on your telephone/internet bills.

16

CYBER CRIME REPORTING PORTAL FOR VICTIMS OF CYBER CRIME:

With extensive use of the Internet for various services, people are becoming victims of cyber-related crime. Various social media platforms (Email, Face book, Instagram, WhatsApp and other chatting sites) have emerged as the most preferred and quickest mode of communication. In order to provide a central platform for registration of cyber-related crimes for women Ministry of Home affairs, Government of India has launched a separate Cyber Crime Reporting Portal for Victims of Cyber Crime.

This portal is an initiative of Government of India under National Mission for the safety of women by utilising Nirbhaya funds, to facilitate victims/complainants to report cybercrime complaints online. At present this portal caters to complaints pertaining to online Child Pornography (CP)/ Child Sexual Abuse Material (CSAM) or sexually explicit content such as Rape/Gang Rape (CP/RGR) content. Complaints reported on this portal are dealt by respective police authorities of States/ UTs based on the information in the complaints provided by the complainants. Option for anonymous reporting of CP/RGR content has been provided on this portal as per the direction of Hon'ble Supreme Court under the matter of Suo Moto Writ Petition no.3/2015 where complainants are not required to disclose their identity

What kind of information, will I have to provide for reporting my complaint?

In case of anonymous complaints - you do not need to provide any personal information. However, information related to the incident / complaint should be complete for the police authorities to take necessary action. In case you opt for "Report and Track" option - Information fields with a red asterisk marks (*) are mandatory. It is very important that the police authorities receive complete information related to the complaint. Therefore, you will need to provide key information such as your name, phone number, email address, details of the incident/ complaint and necessary information supporting the complaint, etc. You will need to register yourself using your mobile number. You will receive a One Time Password (OTP) that will be used to verify your phone number. The OTP is valid for 30 minutes. Once you successfully register your mobile number on the portal, you will be able to report the compliant.

Which state shall I select while reporting an incident/ complaint?

When reporting an Anonymous complaint, the victims' location/ state where the incident has happened should be selected. If it is a report pertaining to website hosting CP/RGR content, complainant can select his/her state.In case you are reporting a complaint through the "Report and Track" option, you may either choose your location (If you are victim) or the victim's location/ state where the incident has happened. As a responsible citizen you should use "Report and Track" option for reporting the incident/ crime, since it would help the Law enforcement agencies to contact you for further details. (Source: Website of Ministry of Home Affairs, Government of India)

For more details go to
https://cybercrime.gov.in/cybercitizen/home.htm#

17

HOW TO CURB TEEN SUICIDES

On April 3, 2017, Arjun Bharadwaj, a 24-year-old management student, committed suicide by jumping out of a 19th-floor hotel room in Mumbai. Media reporting suggested he had been depressed about failure in exams and repeatedly talked about ending his life on social media. There were also suggestions he was battling drug addiction. We come across several such cases. In 2015, the number of student suicides stood at 8,934. In the five years leading to 2015, 39,775 students killed themselves. The number of attempted suicides, many unreported, is likely to be much higher. India has one of the world's highest suicide rates for youth aged 15 to 29, according to a 2012 *Lancet* report.

Suicide is committed by any individual when he does not feel part of himself, his peer group, family and ultimately society. Suicides happen due to various reasons. They don't happen in a day. Every child reflects unusual signs before committing suicide. There is a need to identify these signs in the child by the teachers and parents. Following tips may help in reducing the cases of suicides:

- Parents need to interact regularly with their children. Healthy connect is the core of parent child relationship.
- Working couples need to spare time daily as per their convenience for their children.
- Try to understand his/her anxiety, problems in schools/ workplace.
- Hear the problems of the child with an element of empathy and compassion.
- Always encourage and appreciate his good work and achievements.
- Don't condemn or humiliate the child publicly or in the presence of his peer group for his mistakes.
- Introvert children need a friend, philosopher and guide in their parents.
- Try to identify abnormal behavior in your child and take remedial measures without offending him or humiliating.
- Irritability, talking less, keeping aloof, talking less, giving short answers are some early signs of child under stress.
- Try to identify hidden talent of child and promote it.
- Regularly interact with your child when he/she is appearing for exams and help him/her overcome his anxiety.
- Be equally supportive in their success and failures at different stages of life.
- Try to inculcate good values in the child.
- Expose them to healthy conversations, audios, videos and print literature.

- Fix up timings for his interaction on TV, social media and mobile phone.
- Plan annual family excursion trips with children.

Always remember: A child needs more than a swanky phone and beautiful clothes. Love, compassion, empathy, encouragement, appreciation and constant motivation will always reduce suicidal tendencies in the youth and children.

18

WHAT CREDIT CARD USERS NEED TO WATCH OUT FOR

Credit cards are now commonly used for shopping, at restaurants, for buying movie tickets and so many other things. However, it is important to keep your card carefully and never delay to report its loss as the consequences can prove to be disastrous.

- Lodge a complaint with the bank immediately if you lose your credit card. It will enable the bank to announce it as a 'hot card' as early as possible, thus enabling the authorities to catch the culprit. This will also protect you from liabilities that may be incurred if the stolen card is used.
- Do not write the PIN number on the card itself.

- Always check your monthly bank statements for any suspicious transactions.
- A card's magnetic strip has the basic details of the cardholder. But the card also comes with a blank space for you to sign in. You must sign on the card to avoid unauthorised use.
- Make sure you look at the card when it is being swiped.
- Disable your credit card account if you are not using it.
- Do not store your personal and credit card information on your computer.
- Thoroughly check the authenticity of the firm, the website or any other transactional society where your money would be flowing through.

19

PRECAUTIONS THAT WOMEN SHOULD OBSERVE

Apart from trafficking of women and minor children for sexual exploitation, women can also be victims of crime at their workplace or be subjected to dowry harassment and other forms of cruelty after marriage.

According to *Crime in India 2016*, a total of 3,38,954 cases were committed against women under various sections of law. Cruelty by husband and relatives topped the list with 1,10,378, followed by assault on women with intent to outrage modesty with 84,746 cases, kidnapping and abduction 64,519 and 38,947 cases of rape. As compared to 2015 it registered an increase of 2.9%.

- Be aware of yourself, the surroundings and the probable situations that might affect you.
- It is better to avoid a situation or a place where you have serious apprehensions regarding your safety.
- Try to escape from a situation if you are in the process of forcibly being kidnapped or assaulted. Yell for help at the top of your voice.
- During the process of escape do not hesitate to hurt the assaulter on his vital organs such as the eyes, the groin and so on.
- While driving a car, lock all the doors and keep the windows up to avoid forcible carjacking. Do not open the window at intersections unless the person is known. Do not give a lift to anyone unless you have established the identity of the person.
- If you sense a problem while driving, try changing the route.
- Never take a fixed route for going to office, the market or for a walk.
- Avoid wearing heavy jewellery, particularly if you are walking on the streets.
- Do not take a window seat if travelling by bus so as to avoid easy blockade. Aisle seats are better for escape.
- After peak hours try not to board a bus or a train compartment which has very few people.
- Try to avoid using music systems and gadgets if you are walking on the street.
- Keep your eyes and ears open for suspicious things around you.
- Try to walk with a group in unsafe places, till you reach the safety point.
- Park your car close to the entrance, particularly if you are out shopping at night.
- Watch out for those pretending to be disabled.
- If you are followed by someone while driving, keep track of his movement through the rear view mirror. Do not go to the

predetermined destination. Try to stop near a market or crowded place to avoid the follower.

- Several city police such as the Delhi Police organise self-defence camps for women and college/school-going girls. Be a part of such camps.
- Try to avoid subways, particularly if you are alone at night.

20

PRECAUTIONS THAT CHILDREN NEED TO TAKE

The breakdown of the joint family, the concept of nuclear families and the culture of working couples have made children vulnerable. The magnitude of crime against them at a national level is indeed shocking.

- Make sure you know your full name, telephone number and address.
- Never be alone at your property. Stay with friends even when going to public lavatories.
- Always get your parents' consent before going anywhere and telephone your mother or father often to tell them where you are.

- Walk only on routes to school and elsewhere that your parents have scouted out with you. Never walk through parking lots or take other shortcuts.
- Be alert and do not wear headphones or play hand-held games when walking on the street.
- If someone comes up to you and asks you a question, do not speak to him other than saying, 'Go ask an adult.'
- Never go too near a car or a truck if you are alone. Just run towards other people.
- Cute animals and sweets are two tricks often used by criminals to get close to you.
- Always get your parent's consent before accepting money or a gift from an unknown person.
- If you see someone doing something wrong, just go in the other direction.
- Give up your valuables if you are robbed by someone—never fight back.
- Never get money for any school or club project unless one of your parents is with you.
- Do not trust anyone who tries to get you to break your parents' rules.
- Tell your parents about places or people who make you feel unsafe.
- Have a secret code word for emergencies. If you telephone your parents while you are with someone who scares you, you can utter the code word to secretly let your parents know that you need help.

21

PREVENTING TRAFFICKING OF CHILDREN

Often minor girls are procured by unscrupulous persons by giving false hopes of lucrative jobs in the country as well as abroad. These girls are then pushed into prostitution or other illegal activities. Most of the victims are from poor families in backward states. Care should be taken by the parents of such victims. According to *Crime in India 2016*, a total of 17,876 children (male and female) were trafficked in the country below the age of 18 years (p. 513).

- Verify any offers of jobs for your minor daughters.
- Try to get concrete details about their prospective employers.

- Try to get in touch with the employer directly without informing the local middlemen.
- Never allow your child to go alone to a city with an unknown person.
- Your child should always be accompanied by an elder member of the family.

22

HOW TO PROCURE GENUINE DOCUMENTS

Various identity documents such as Aadhar, PAN card, passport, driving licence and so on are required for availing different facilities. Quite often unscrupulous persons promise to deliver these to us quickly and we get tempted to get the work done by them. But remember that several gangs specialise in preparing fake documents which, in the long run, turn out to be bogus.

- Always access the official and certified websites of the agencies.
- Approach only the authorised and registered agents or representatives of these organisations.

- Establish their identity through photo ID cards.
- Crosscheck with their employers.
- Do not approach touts or middlemen loitering around such offices for help.
- Never hand over your crucial and vital details to unauthorised persons as the information could be misused.

23

HANDLING FALSE JOB PROMISES

Getting a job today has become a necessity for both men and women. This can be done through word-of-mouth or via advertisements in the print and visual media. However, many fall into the trap of false job promises. Take the following tips to avoid such an experience:

- Be careful of advertisements or individuals offering overseas jobs. Check their antecedents.
- Check the website of the companies that are offering these jobs.

- Do not hesitate to approach the consulate of the country concerned for any help.
- Before complaining, contact the official organisations to check about the employers.
- Never handover your valid travel documents to unauthorised persons for getting visas or tickets.
- Do not handover cash to middlemen or unauthorised persons for getting things done.
- Make all payments by cheque.
- Do not handover blank or post-dated cheques.

24

WHAT TO WATCH OUT FOR WHEN DRIVING A CAR

Driving your own car to work or elsewhere is common today. With rising salaries, even young people, both girls and boys, drive their own cars. But remember that a friendly knock could be fatal...

- Keep the windows rolled up and doors locked.
- Never roll down the window at the request of a stranger.
- Avoid keeping costly items on the dashboard or on the rear seat.
- Do not give a lift to someone you do not know.
- Roll up the windows while waiting at a read light to avoid the theft of items such as mobile phones and so on.

25

PRECAUTIONS FOR VICTIMS OF CRIME

Every criminal leaves a clue behind after committing a crime. Initial clues left by a criminal play a very important role in solving a crime. It is on the basis of these that a criminal can be arrested by the police. The next important role is played by the victims. At times the most vital clues are tampered by the victims themselves owing to ignorance and panic.

- Make a hue and cry and inform the local police immediately through the fastest means of communication if any crime has taken place on the street or inside your house.
- You, as well as the other inmates of the house, should not touch any article in the house till the arrival of the police, particularly in cases of house theft and burglary.

- You should help the police in locating articles that do not belong to the house. An attempt should be to identify foreign elements at the scene of the crime.
- If you have come in physical contact with the criminal or seen him leaving the scene of crime, provide as many details regarding his physical features and other characteristics as possible.

- If the criminal has escaped on a vehicle, try to note down the company, number and colour of the vehicle.
- Try to recollect and remember all details, however insignificant, and pass these on to the police.
- Do not allow friends, onlookers or inmates to touch or disturb the scene of crime.
- Do not touch glasses, tumblers, bottles, cupboards or shelves as these could contain fingerprints and other valuable clues.
- If there is blood at the scene of crime do not clean it without the permission of the police.
- Isolate the area where the crime has been committed if it is inside the house and keep it out of bounds for children, inmates and sympathisers.
- If a crime has been committed inside a motor vehicle, do not touch it till the police arrive. It could contain fingerprints.

26

THINK TWICE BEFORE PLAYING THESE DEADLY GAMES

BLUE WHALE GAME

Blue whale Challenge, known as a popular game on the Internet, came to light in the year 2016 in Russia with the death of few teenaged youths. Any participant in the game is assigned a series of tasks to be performed within a period of 50 days. As soon as a player gradually clears various challenges he is cornered to a situation at the end and motivated to do physical harm including suicide. It is also believed that in 2016, Philipp Budeikin, a 21-year-old former psychology student who was expelled from his university, claimed that he invented the game in 2013. He said his intention was to cleanse society by pushing persons whom he deemed as having no value to suicide.

Since 2016 the game became very popular in the West and lot of youths became victim of the game and committed suicide. In 2017 several teens became victim of this game in India. Accordingly due to lot public outcry and government intervention various Internet sites were forced to ban the link of this site. With conflicting claims regarding the existence of the game Ministry of Home affairs came out with advisories, followed by massive awareness campaign by the schools and law enforcing agencies.

MOMO CHALLENGE

What is Momo

The game started in Mexico, with players "challenged" to communicate on WhatsApp with an unknown person known as Momo, according to the Computer Crime Investigation Unit of the State of Tabasco, Mexico.

The avatar used by Momo on the app is an image of a woman with bulging eyes and black hair. The disturbing picture was initially believed to show a work by Japanese artist Midori Hayashi, but is actually of a sculpture created by Japanese special effects company Link Factory and displayed at a Tokyo gallery. However neither the company nor Hayashi had anything to do with the Momo challenge, which began being shared online in August 2016,

Users who engage with Momo on WhatsApp are sent disturbing and graphic photographs. In some cases they are 'doxed' into self-harm and suicide. Doxing "is when someone hacks your private information and then threatens to share it online or in a public forum, akin to blackmail".

As soon as this game started spreading in India, Central Board of Secondary Education intervened with advisories to take effective measures against the use of this game in children followed by massive awareness campaign by the law enforcing agencies.

Precautions:

- Various studies have shown that lot of children are becoming victims of cyber-related crimes including addiction to such games due to peer pressure, lack of parental control and regulatory mechanisms in schools.
- There is a need for parents to devote more time with the children and engage them in meaningful interactions in day-to-day life so that they don't become victims of such deadly games.
- Don't share your personal information like name, date of birth, address and phone numbers with players while playing a game.

- Never share your parent's credit card/debit card details with any one while interacting in the game.
- Never install/download games from unknown free online gaming websites which are not well known.
- Never download games by clicking on the links communicated to you through emails. It might contain viruses and malwares which could affect the security of your computer or mobile devices.
- Never use voice chats or web cam while playing games. This exposes you to other unknown cyber criminals who could indulge in other cyber-related activities.
- Never meet in person with someone from your online gaming world. In real life he may not be the same with whom you have been interacting online.
- Don't hesitate to share your problems with your parents and friends.
- Never follow instructions blindly on the Internet without realizing the consequences.

ABOUT THE AUTHOR

O.P. Mishra is a serving Indian Police Service Officer of the AGMUT Cadre. A PhD in sociology from Jawaharlal Nehru University, New Delhi, he has written for Indian Police journal and contributed chapters in various edited books including course materials for various courses of Indira Gandhi National Open University. His book, *Policing Delhi: Urbanization, Crime and Law Enforcement* is an important contribution towards understanding the sociology of crime in the metropolitan city. The officer is credited with introducing several reforms in the prison as IG Prisons Chandigarh, which were incorporated in the coffee table book: *Turning A New Leaf: Redefining Prison Administration and Management.* Apart from serving in A&N Islands, Delhi, Goa and Chandigarh, he has also served as International Civil Police Officer in United Nations Mission in Kosovo. Dr Mishra has distinguished himself as an ace investigator, effective strategist and tactful law and order handler with operational expertise and professional acumen in planning and executing mega security arrangements. He is a recipient of President's Police Medal for Meritorious Services and President's Police Medal for Distinguished Services.